Healing Scriptures

For

Peace & Comfort

Bible: King James Version (KJV)

Carrie Payne

Healing Scriptures
For
Peace & Comfort

Bible: King James Version (KJV)

❧Dedication❧

I would like to dedicate this book to my Mother, her Guardian Angel and anyone in need of a boost in faith, hope, love, and awe of the beauty in this world.

Carrie Payne, Thurmont, Maryland

All Scriptures are taken from the
KING JAMES VERSION (KJV):
KING JAMES VERSION, public domain

1st Edition
ISBN-13: 978-1544923802 (CreateSpace)
ISBN-10: 1544923805
Copyright 2017
All Rights Reserved
Printed in United States of America
Order Book: www.amazon.com
Book Publisher: www.createspace.com

Author's Note: The following Bible Scriptures are accompanied by photography taken by my Mom.

❧Through God all things are possible, *even* the improbable and the unimaginable. He gives us hope.❧

This book was inspired solely by my mother and her beautiful photography. She has always been a wonderful example of love, perseverance, happiness, determination, strength and so much more. My Mom has overcome many obstacles and always has done so with a smile. (Maybe a few grumbles too, but she is human).

The first trial was divorce. She separated at a young age with a small child, at a time when divorce was not the norm and not accepted by her church. A decade later Mom was diagnosed with endometriosis and had to have a hysterectomy.

A couple of years ago, two months after a clear mammogram, Mom discovered a hard pea size lump. After a visit with her doctor, she was diagnosed with breast cancer. She had three surgeries to remove the tumor which ended in a partial, but successful, mastectomy. Mom was very strong during the whole ordeal, from the diagnosis to the follow up visit that announced her cancer free. There were many prayers of gratitude for sparing her life and ridding her of cancer.

If that wasn't enough to overcome, two months later, she and her husband were cutting down trees to prepare for winter, as they had done for many years. Unfortunately, there was a terrible accident and Mom was hit by a falling tree. She sustained many injuries and was in ICU for a week, fighting for her life. (It was the scariest week of my life and fortunately for Mom, she doesn't remember this part). She was instantly paralyzed, and remains so, but continues with hope, faith, and determination to walk again one day. This has been the toughest challenge of all for my mother, but she continues to smile and doesn't let her paralysis stop her from enjoying life!

Mom called me one day and proposed the idea of writing a scripture inspired book revolving around her healing and photography. I knew at that moment that I wanted nothing more than to make that a reality for her.

"Mom, Thank you! For being an example of faith through every trial. Love you!"

Carrie

❧ From the Photographer ❧

As a child, I grew up in a large, loving family where prayer was a part of our daily living. Once I left home, things changed and my prayers got shorter. I usually just thanked God for a wonderful day, even if it turned out not to be one. As I got older, I encountered other life altering occurrences. Each had a different effect on me. The most recent one brought me closer to God and back to my faith.

God has a purpose for everyone, although I'm still not sure about mine. He spared my life, from breast cancer, and if that wasn't enough, he spared my life again when a falling tree struck me. While recovering from all my injuries, my family told me about all the people who were praying for me; it was truly humbling. People from different beliefs and religious backgrounds were praying for me to get up and walk again. It changed my life in many ways and made my faith in God even stronger.

A visit with my Aunt Sarah, and her family, whom I had not seen in many years, made my faith even more complete. As we visited, Aunt Sarah mentioned that she had a list of healing scriptures from the Bible, and if I would like a copy. Of course, I said "Yes". I never thought of referring to the Bible or scriptures for healing. When I got home I found the Bible my parents had given to my family several years earlier for Christmas and dusted it off. I marked each scripture and used sticky notes for easy reference. I was truly amazed after reading the scriptures as they brought much peace and comfort to me. The Bible has allowed me to be more accepting of what has happened to me, and has given me the hope I need to walk again one day.

Thus, I was inspired to go through all the many pictures, I have taken over the years and do something creative with them. Some were chosen for what I thought were relevant for that specific scripture. Others I chose because I liked the picture. Read them and see if you can figure out why that picture was used. Ask yourself, "What was the person on the top of the sand dune thinking as they were just about to the top?" Or, "What was the person feeling, while walking on the narrow swinging bridge over the rushing water below?" "How can I relate to this specific picture, but more importantly, apply this scripture to my life?"

Only God knows!

I hope this book gives you peace & comfort during trying times.

Carries
Mom
Sue B

4

Table of Contents

Montana, South Island Lake area

Mark 11:22-24

"And Jesus answering saith unto them,
Have faith in God.
For verily I say unto you,
That whosoever shall say unto this mountain,
Be thou removed, and be thou cast into the sea;
And shall not doubt in his heart,
but shall believe that those things which he saith
shall come to pass; he shall have whatsoever he saith.
Therefore, I say unto you,
what things soever ye desire, when ye pray,
believe that ye receive them and ye shall have them."

Psalm 107:19-20

"Then they cry unto the LORD in their trouble,
and he saveth them out of their distresses.
He sent his word,
and healed them,
and delivered them from their destructions."

Nevada, Rhyolite ghost town near Beatty

North Dakota, A frosty morning sunrise

Isaiah 58:8

"Then shall thy light break forth as the morning,
and thine health shall spring forth speedily:
and thy righteousness shall go before thee;
the glory of the LORD shall be thy rereward."

3 John 1:2

"Beloved,
I wish above all things
that thou mayest prosper
and be in health,
even as thy soul
prospereth."

Utah, Three Sisters at Arches National Park near town of Moab

Utah, Burr Trail Scenic Backway starts in town of Boulder

Matthew 8:13

" And Jesus said unto the centurion,
Go thy way;
and as thou hast believed,
so be it done unto thee.
And his servant was healed in the selfsame hour."

Isaiah 53:5

"But he was wounded for our transgressions,
he was bruised for our iniquities:
the chastisement of our peace was upon him;
and with his stripes we are healed"

Utah, Paria town site area of Grand Staircase-Escalante National Monument

Utah, Twin Rocks located in town of Bluff

Matthew 18:19

"Again I say unto you,
That if two of you shall agree on earth as touching
any thing that they shall ask,
it shall be done for them of my
Father which is in heaven."

John 16:23-24

" And in that day ye shall ask me nothing.
Verily, verily, I say unto you,
Whatsoever ye shall ask the Father in my name,
he will give it you.
Hitherto have ye asked nothing in my name:
ask, and ye shall receive, that your joy may be full."

Oregon, Tide Pool on a beach along the Pacific Ocean

Isaiah 57:19

"I create the fruit of the lips;
Peace, peace to him that is far off,
and to him that is near,
saith the LORD;
and I will heal him."

California, Mesquite Flat Sand Dunes north west of Death Valley

Matthew 8:16-17

"When the even was come,
they brought unto him many
that were possessed with devils:
and he cast out the spirits with his word,
and healed all that were sick:
That it might be fulfilled which was spoken by
Esaias the prophet, saying,
Himself took our infirmities, and bare our sicknesses."

Nevada, Whitney Pockets, sandstone eroded along remote area of Gold Butte Rd.

Oregon, A spot near town of Bandon on the Pacific Ocean

Romans 4:17

"As it is written,
I have made thee a father of many nations,
before him whom he believed,
even God,
who quickeneth the dead,
and calleth those things which
be not as though they were."

Isaiah 41:10

"Fear thou not; for I am with thee:
be not dismayed; for I am thy God:
I will strengthen thee; yea,
I will help thee; yea,
I will uphold thee with the right hand
of my righteousness."

Arizona, Hawk in the desert

Jeremiah 33:6

"Behold, I will bring it health and cure,
and I will cure them,
and will reveal unto them the
abundance of peace and truth."

Colorado, Corn Field

John 14:13-14

"And whatsoever ye shall ask in my name,
that will I do,
that the Father may be glorified in the Son.
If ye shall ask any thing in my name.
I will do it."

Oregon, Fall Reflections

Luke 6:19

" And the whole multitude sought to touch him:
For there went virtue out of him,
and healed them all."

Oregon, Beach on the Pacific Ocean

Psalm 42:11

"Why art thou cast down,
O my soul?
and why art thou
disquieted within me?
hope thou in God:
for I shall yet praise him,
who is the health of my
countenance,
and my God."

California, Fort Point in San Francisco

Utah, San Rafael Swell area near Castle Rock

Matthew 4:23-24

"And Jesus went about all Galilee,
teaching in their synagogues, and preaching
the gospel of the kingdom,
and healing all manner of sickness
and all manner of disease among the people.
And his fame went throughout all Syria:
and they brought unto him all sick people that were
taken with divers diseases and torments,
and those which were possessed with devils,
and those which were lunatick,
and those that had the palsy;
and he healed them."

James 5:14-15

"Is any sick among you?
Let him call for the elders of the church;
and let them pray over him,
anointing him with oil in the name of the Lord:
and the prayer of faith shall save the sick,
and the Lord shall raise him up;
and if he have committed sins,
they shall be forgiven him. "

Utah, Church Rock is north of town of Monticello on Rt. 191

1 Peter 2:24

"Who his own self
bare our sins
in his own body
on the tree,
that we,
being dead to sins,
should live unto
righteousness:
by whose stripes
ye were healed."

California, Lone Pine Tree

Proverbs 17:22

"A merry heart
doeth good like
a medicine:
but a broken spirit
drieth the bones."

California, Death Valley - Bad water area

Jeremiah 30:17

" For I will restore health unto thee,
and I will heal thee of thy wounds,
saith the LORD;
because they called thee an Outcast,
saying, This is Zion,
whom no man seeketh after."

Utah, Zion National Park near town of Springdale

Psalm 6:1-10

Holy Cloud

"O LORD, rebuke me not in thine anger, neither chasten me in thy hot displeasure. Have mercy upon me, O LORD; for I am weak: O LORD, heal me; for my bones are vexed. My soul is also sore vexed: but thou, O LORD, how long? Return, O LORD, deliver my soul: oh save me for thy mercies' sake. For in death there is no remembrance of thee: in the grave who shall give thee thanks? I am weary with my groaning; all the night I make my bed to swim; I water my couch with my tears. Mine eye is consumed because of grief; it waxeth old because of all mine enemies. Depart from me, all ye workers of iniquity; for the LORD hath heard the voice of my weeping. The LORD hath heard my supplication; the LORD will receive my prayer. Let all mine enemies be ashamed and sore vexed: let them return and be ashamed suddenly."

Proverbs 4:20-24

"My son, attend to my words;
incline thine ear unto my sayings.
Let them not depart from thine eyes;
keep them in the midst of thine heart.
For they are life unto those that find them,
and health to all their flesh.
Keep thy heart with all diligence;
for out of it are the issues of life.
Put away from thee a froward mouth,
and perverse lips put far from thee."

Montana, Kootenai River gorge suspension bridge
(Look closely on right of bridge for a person about to cross)

Jeremiah 17:14

"Heal me,
O LORD,
and I shall be healed;
save me,
and I shall be saved:
for thou art my praise."

Utah, Devil's Garden, near Escalante

Michigan, Lake Superior rocky beach

Psalms 25:17-18

"The troubles of my heart are enlarged:
O bring thou me out of my distresses.
Look upon mine affliction and my pain;
and forgive all my sins."

Utah, Newspaper Rock State Historic Monument

Mark 16:17-18

"And these signs shall follow them that believe;
In my name shall they cast out devils;
they shall speak with new tongues;
They shall take up serpents;
and if they drink any deadly thing,
it shall not hurt them;
they shall lay hands on the sick,
and they shall recover."

1 Thessalonians 5:23

"And the very God of peace sanctify you wholly;
and I pray God your whole spirit and soul and body
be preserved blameless unto the coming of our
Lord Jesus Christ."

Utah, Hovenweep National Monument

John 8:36

"If the Son therefore shall
make you free,
ye shall be free indeed."

Michigan, Ice on a calm Lake Superior

Matthew 21:14

Oregon, Beach

"And the blind and the lame
came to him in the temple;
and he healed them."

Malachi 4:2

"But unto you that fear my name
shall the Sun of righteousness arise
with healing in his wings;
and ye shall go forth,
and grow up as calves of the stall."

Utah, Devil's Garden arch – Angel Wings

Exodus 23:25

"And ye shall serve the LORD your God,
and he shall bless thy bread,
and thy water;
and I will take sickness away from the midst of thee."

Michigan, Lake Superior – Little Presque Island area near Marquette

Arizona, Casa Grande Ruins National Monument

Matthew 8:5-8

"And when Jesus was entered into Capernaum,
there came unto him a centurion,
beseeching him, and saying, Lord,
my servant lieth at home sick of the palsy,
grievously tormented. And Jesus saith unto him,
I will come and heal him.
The centurion answered and said,
Lord, I am not worthy that thou shouldest come
under my roof: but speak the word only,
and my servant shall be healed."

Isaiah 54: 4-5

"Fear not; for thou shalt not be ashamed:
neither be thou confounded;
for thou shalt not be put to shame:
for thou shalt forget the shame of thy youth,
and shalt not remember the reproach
of thy widowhood any more.
For thy Maker is thine husband;
the LORD of hosts is his name;
and thy Redeemer the Holy One of Israel;
The God of the whole earth shall he be called."

Arizona, Saguaro Cactus Bloom

Lonely Dead Tree

Isaiah 38:16

"O Lord, by these things men live,
and in all these things is the life of my spirit:
so wilt thou recover me, and make me to live."

Job 4:3-4

"Behold,
thou hast instructed many,
and thou hast strengthened
the weak hands.
Thy words have upholden
him that was falling,
and thou hast strengthened
the feeble knees."

Philippians 4:7

"And the peace of God,
which passeth all
understanding,
shall keep your hearts
and minds through
Christ Jesus."

Inside of Yellow Rose

Utah, San Rafael Swell Area – Mother Daughter Rock

Matthew 15:28

"Then Jesus answered and said unto her,
O woman, great is thy faith:
be it unto thee even as thou wilt.
And her daughter was made whole
from that very hour."

Luke 4:40

"Now when the sun was setting,
all they that had any sick
with divers diseases
brought them unto him;
and he laid his hands
on every one of them,
and healed them."

Arizona, person watching the sunset

Proverbs: 3:7-8

"Be not wise in thine own eyes: fear the LORD, and depart from evil. It shall be health to thy navel, and marrow to thy bones."

California, Bodie State Park – Ghost Town

Psalm 91:15-16

"He shall call upon me,
and I will answer him:
I will be with him in trouble;
I will deliver him,
and honour him.
With long life will I satisfy him,
and shew him my salvation."

Hummingbird

Colorado, Old Railroad Bridge

Romans 8:11

"But if the Spirit of him that raised up
Jesus from the dead dwell in you,
he that raised up Christ from the dead
shall also quicken your mortal bodies
by his Spirit that dwelleth in you."

Utah, Bryce Canyon National Park

Matthew 15:30

"And great multitudes came unto him,
having with them those that were lame,
blind, dumb, maimed, and many others,
and cast them down at Jesus' feet;
and he healed them:"

Luke 9:11

And the people, when they knew it,
followed him: and he received them,
and spake unto them of the kingdom of God,
and healed them that had need of healing.

Full Moon at Sunset

Utah, Valley of the gods located near its southern border

Ephesians 6:10

"Finally, my brethren,
be strong in the Lord,
and in the power of his might."

My Father's Love

The Last Supper

Edgar Lantzer

It happened that these panels were at St. Peters Cathedral, in Upper Michigan, while my Mom and I were visiting there. We went to see them; I was awestruck when I took pictures of these panels, wanting to learn more about the inspiring artist, and bring to light the testament of one man's faith!

"My Father's Love"

Edgar Lantzer developed scarlet fever as a child and it affected his brain, unable to write but able to read. So, "Ed's" father taught him Marquetry (the art of putting small pieces of wood over another wood to form a picture). What sets his work apart from others is there were no sketches, he simply created. Each diamond shaped piece was cut identically and made of different woods. Most of his wood was found in dumpsters as he was homeless. Ed devoted his later life to making these masterpieces, a total of thirty, 4'x8' panels. The Last Supper is made up of seven panels and all lining up perfectly when put together. How could this be? It's a true gift from his father and his Heavenly Father. His story is amazing.

Carrie's Mom

To learn more about Edgar Lantzer go to: www.myfatherslove.info
Or read "Mural Writer" by LaShelle VanHouten (available on amazon.com)

Made in the USA
Monee, IL
29 September 2024

66214793R00026